Dog Groups
Non-Sporting Group

by Julie Murray

Dash!
LEVELED READERS
An Imprint of Abdo Zoom • abdobooks.com

Level 1 – Beginning
Short and simple sentences with familiar words or patterns for children who are beginning to understand how letters and sounds go together.

Level 2 – Emerging
Longer words and sentences with more complex language patterns for readers who are practicing common words and letter sounds.

Level 3 – Transitional
More developed language and vocabulary for readers who are becoming more independent.

abdobooks.com

Published by Abdo Zoom, a division of ABDO, PO Box 398166, Minneapolis, Minnesota 55439. Copyright © 2024 by Abdo Consulting Group, Inc. International copyrights reserved in all countries. No part of this book may be reproduced in any form without written permission from the publisher. Dash!™ is a trademark and logo of Abdo Zoom.

Printed in the United States of America, North Mankato, Minnesota.
102023
012024

Photo Credits: Getty Images, Shutterstock
Production Contributors: Jennie Forsberg, Grace Hansen
Design Contributors: Candice Keimig, Neil Klinepier

Library of Congress Control Number: 2023938007

Publisher's Cataloging in Publication Data
Names: Murray, Julie, author.
Title: Non-Sporting group / by Julie Murray
Description: Minneapolis, Minnesota : Abdo Zoom, 2024 | Series: Dog groups | Includes online resources and index.
Identifiers: ISBN 9781098284039 (lib. bdg.) | ISBN 9781098284756 (eBook) | ISBN 9781098285111 (Read-to-Me eBook)
Subjects: LCSH: Pets--Juvenile literature. | Dog breeds--Juvenile literature. | Dogs--Juvenile literature. | Dogs--Behavior--Juvenile literature.
Classification: DDC 636.72--dc23

Table of Contents

Non-Sporting Group 4

Characteristics 10

More Non-Sporting Breeds . . 22

Glossary 23

Index 24

Online Resources 24

Non-Sporting Group

The Non-Sporting Group is made up of 21 dog **breeds**. It is one of the original dog groups of the American Kennel Club (AKC).

Bulldog

French Bulldog

The group contains **breeds** of all sizes, talents, and backgrounds.

Many of the **breeds** in this group were **bred** for a specific job. Today, they no longer do these jobs.

Characteristics

10

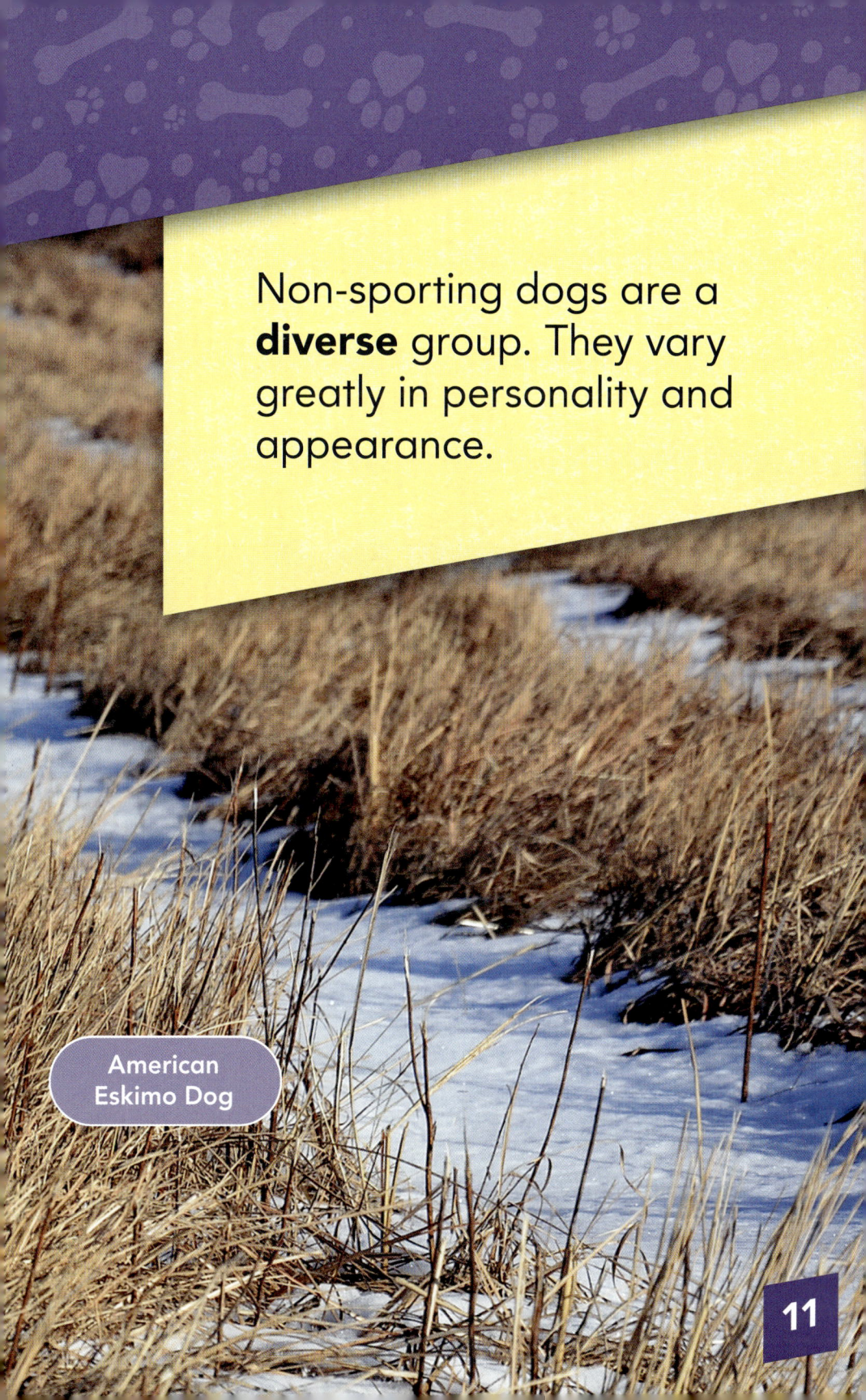

Non-sporting dogs are a **diverse** group. They vary greatly in personality and appearance.

American Eskimo Dog

Non-sporting dogs are smart. Most are easy to train. They like to learn tricks.

Poodle (Standard)

Dogs in this group are often playful. They enjoy fetch and other games.

Some can be **wary** of strangers. Others are comfortable with everyone.

Chow Chow

They are loving and **loyal** dogs. Most do well with children and other animals.

Shiba Inu

Non-sporting dogs make great pets. They are often called companion dogs.

Boston Terrier

More Non-Sporting Breeds

Bichon Frise

Chinese Shar-Pei

Finnish Spitz

Lhasa Apso

Poodle (Miniature)

Schipperke

22

Glossary

bred – developed over time for a certain purpose.

breed – a particular type of animal.

diverse – of different kinds or sorts.

loyal – showing devotion and faithfulness to someone or something.

wary – on guard or showing caution.

Index

American Kennel Club 4

appearance 7, 11

intelligence 12

personality 11, 15, 16, 19

play 15

size 11

training 12

tricks 12

Online Resources

To learn more about the Non-Sporting Group, please visit **abdobooklinks.com** or scan this QR code. These links are routinely monitored and updated to provide the most current information available.